MARIE CLEMONS

God's Money Moves for Women

A Guide to Biblical Wealth, Debt-Free Living, and Purpose-Driven Finances

First published by Clemons & Co. Publishing 2025

Copyright © 2025 by Marie Clemons

First edition

ISBN: 979-8-218-66875-4

This book was professionally typeset on Reedsy.
Find out more at reedsy.com

Contents

V   Part Five

Introduction

From Broke and Burdened to Bold and Biblical

Let me start by saying I'm not here as some financial expert or religious professional—just someone who's been there.

I didn't write this book because I've always had it together.

I wrote it because *I didn't.*

I'm your regular every day wife and mom who realized one day that there was a better way.

I know what it feels like to watch the bills stack up, to not have enough, and the confusing feeling of wanting to honor God but feeling financially stuck.

I know the frustration of working hard, trying to do right, and still wondering, *"Why am I not further along by now?"*

I also know what it's like to carry that quietly—showing up strong while privately wondering how to stretch a paycheck, repair a mistake, or break free from a cycle I kept repeating.

But the deeper I went into my faith, I realized I had to start asking different questions.

Not *"How can I get more money?"* but:

"What does God actually say about this?"

"Is wealth even something I'm supposed to want?"

Those questions led me down a new path, to a new truth. Truth that was buried under layers of fear, shame, bad teaching, and survival mentality. Truth that shifted everything.

And now, I'm here to share it with you.

This Book Is For You If…

- You're tired of struggling and ready to take control of your money
- You're ready to walk the path towards financial freedom with principles backed by faith—no judgment, no fluff
- You're ready to walk in your purpose, embrace peace, and receive provision

This isn't a book filled with graphs and guilt trips.

It's a guidebook. A story. A mirror. A tool. A companion.

Each chapter will combine:

- **Scripture** - because the Word is our guide
- **Stories** - because you're not alone in this
- **Steps** - because faith without works is still dead
- **Reflection** + **prayer** - because healing happens with God

You'll find both comfort and challenge in these pages.

I'm not here to overwhelm you—but to walk beside you.

To show you that wealth, in the hands of a woman led by the principles of God, is not just possible—it's *powerful.*

This is your invitation to move from broke and burdened... *to bold and biblical.*

And it starts now.

Let's go.

I

Part One

Breaking the Cycle

"Forget the former things; do not dwell on the past. See, I am doing a new thing! Now it springs up; do you not perceive it?" Isaiah 43:18–19

Chapter 1: Debt Is Slavery – Choose Freedom

Let me tell you something that might sting a little: *debt is bondage.* It's not just a normal part of life.

I know that might sound harsh, but I say it with love—because I've lived it. So trust me I'm not judging you. I know what it's like to fall into the cycle of maxed-out credit cards and buying things I didn't really need. It felt normal. Everyone around me was doing it—credit cards, car loans, personal loans, buy now pay later. It all felt so normal.

But looking back? It wasn't freedom. It was being stuck.

And you know that feeling—that tightness in your chest or the knot in your stomach when you check your account or think about your bills? That's not just stress. That's your body reacting to the pressure of carrying something God never meant for you to hold.

Debt doesn't just mess with your money—it messes with your peace. Your joy. Your future. And if we really want to walk in purpose and experience God's abundance, we have to be honest about what debt is doing—and choose a better way forward.

The Month I Had to Choose Between My Purpose and My Payment

There was a time when an amazing opportunity came my way—one that fit perfectly with my goals and would've helped me grow. Mentally, I was ready. But financially? I was empty.

And the opportunity only cost $800. But there was one problem—I didn't have $800.

What I *did* have was five maxed-out credit cards and a paycheck already claimed by credit card payments, a car loan, and that Buy Now, Pay Later demon.

So what happened? I missed out on something that could've changed my life. But I walked away with a lesson I couldn't ignore: *I had to fix my finances.*

At first, I didn't even understand how I got here. Where was all my money going? I had to be honest with myself and do some serious self-reflecting.

And in the midst of my searching, I picked up my Bible and found the answers to all my questions. I found clarity in the Word. The answer just wasn't what I expected:

He said, *"I already gave you the provision. You just gave it to someone else—with interest."*

Debt Steals More Than Just Money

The more I thought about it, the deeper the message resonated with me. God had already provided me with everything I needed, but I'd given it away... with interest.

And I didn't truly realize it until I missed out on something that really mattered. That $800 opportunity could've helped me grow, challenged me, maybe even pushed me in a new direction. But I wasn't financially ready, and that's what hurt the most. Not the money—but the fact that I had to say no because I wasn't in position.

I realized then that debt doesn't just affect your bank account. It affects your entire life.

It steals your options, keeping you stuck in a job that drains you because the bills say you can't afford to leave. It drains your energy, forcing you to work extra hours or take on side hustles just to stay afloat. It delays your legacy, making it hard to build something lasting when you're still paying off yesterday's choices. And it robs you of peace of mind. Leaving you anxious and constantly on edge, bracing for the next bill, the next overdraft, the next reminder that you're not in control.

That's when it hit me—debt isn't just financial. It's emotional. It's spiritual.

It quietly reshapes your decisions, your relationships, even how you see yourself. And the longer you carry it, the heavier it feels—until you're just trying to survive, not thrive.

And the hardest part?

It makes you so focused on surviving, you can't even hear where God is calling you.

Not because you don't trust Him. But because when He nudges you to move, give, or start something new—you pause. Not out of fear, but because your money is already tied up in things that don't even serve your future.

I had to sit with that. And it changed how I saw everything.

This isn't about shame. It's about recognizing what's really holding us back. And once you see it, you can't unsee it. You can start making different decisions—ones that make room for peace, purpose, and flexibility.

Because the next time something life-changing comes your way? I want you to be able to say yes.

What Scripture Says

God didn't create you to be stuck in a cycle of bills, debt, and barely getting by. Living paycheck to paycheck and calling it "faith" isn't what He had in mind.

- **Proverbs 22:7** - *"The borrower is slave to the lender."* That's not just a figure of speech—it's real. Debt weighs on you. It limits your options, drains your peace, and holds you back from living freely—both financially and spiritually.
- **Romans 13:8** - *"Owe no one anything, except to love one another."* Imagine that—your only obligation being to love people well, not to keep up with payments or interest rates.
- **Psalm 37:21** - *"The wicked borrow and do not repay, but the righteous give generously."* Living generously—giving freely, supporting others—that's part of what it means to live right.

You weren't meant to spend your life trying to catch up. You were called to be the lender, not the one stuck in repayment mode. You were made for generosity, not just getting by.

That debt cycle? That's not the whole story.

Freedom is.

Prayer for Financial Freedom

Lord, I confess that I have not always made wise decisions with money. I've borrowed more than I should, and I've leaned on debt when I should have leaned on You. I ask for your forgiveness and your guidance. Help me to walk in wisdom, discipline, and faith. Give me the strength to break free from every chain of financial bondage and to step into the freedom You've already promised. Amen.

Action Steps

1. **Know what you owe.** Grab a notebook or a notes app. List every debt—credit cards, personal loans, car payments, whatever it is. Don't worry about how big the number feels. This is just about facing it with clarity.
2. **Look at your income vs. expenses.** Where is your money actually going? Not just what you think you're spending, but what's really happening. You can't take control if you don't know the flow.
3. **Pick one small win.** Choose one debt—maybe the smallest one or the one that's bothering you the most—and make a plan to start chipping away at it. Progress builds confidence.
4. **Pause the extra spending.** This isn't about deprivation. It's about being intentional. Ask yourself, "Does this serve where I'm trying to go?" If it doesn't, it can probably wait.
5. **Talk to God about your finances.** It's okay if this feels new. Just be honest. Ask for wisdom, for discipline, for provision. You don't have to do this alone—and you weren't meant to.

Reflection Questions

- What thoughts or emotions come up when you think about your debt?
- When did you first believe that "debt was just part of life"?
- How would your life change if you owed no one? How would it shift your peace, your choices, your future?

Freedom isn't just about money—it's spiritual.
   And the truth is, you can't fully serve both God and debt.
   So now it's time to ask yourself:
   What are you choosing?

Chapter 2: God Cares About Your Budget

Let's be honest—when most people hear the word "budget," they automatically shut down.

I used to be the same way. It felt restrictive, like I was being punished for overspending.

But the truth is, a budget isn't a restriction, it's a *revelation*.

It reveals to you where your money is going.

It reveals to you what you're prioritizing.

And in my case, it revealed that I wasn't taking what God had trusted me with seriously.

What I didn't understand back then is that budgeting isn't just about being "good with money." It's about taking care of what you've been given. It's *stewardship*.

It's a way of saying, *"God, I see what You've given me, and I want to manage it well."*

God isn't asking us to blindly manage our finances .

He's calling us to count the cost, make a plan, and walk with wisdom.

Why We Avoid Budgeting

Let's talk about why so many of us avoid budgeting in the first place.

For some of us, it's fear. We're afraid of what the numbers might show us.

For others, it's a lack of knowledge. We were never really shown how to create a budget that actually works.

And there are also a lot of people who feel that only "rich" people budget.

But if Jesus Himself said *you don't build without first counting the cost*, then why are we building lives, families, and futures without looking at the numbers?

Not budgeting doesn't mean you're free.

It usually just means you're avoiding something.

And avoidance?

It creates cycles that keep repeating—until you finally choose to face them.

The Month I Stopped Guessing

After a string of financial setbacks and watching my account hit zero more times than I'd like to admit, I finally made a decision:

It was time to stop guessing what was in my account and actually sit down to look at the numbers.

And as you probably guessed, it wasn't pretty.

I had more expenses going out than I had income coming in. I was using credit cards to fill in where the income didn't. I had subscriptions for services I had long forgot about and stopped using. There were small purchases that seemed innocent at the time, but had quickly added up. And I was spending entirely too much eating out.

But you know what surprised me the most?

The *peace* I felt when I saw it all clearly.

Facing it gave me clarity. I finally understood what had been holding me back. I could see exactly where things were off—and more importantly, where I could make changes.

The budget became my plan.

And once I had a plan? I didn't feel broke—I felt empowered.

Sometimes we avoid looking at the numbers because we're afraid of what they'll reveal.

But the truth is: clarity is the first step to change.

You can't fix what you won't face.

And you can't build financial peace on a foundation of avoidance.

When you budget, you give your money direction, you allow room for growth.

You become intentional with your life.

What Scripture Says

Let's anchor this in truth—because the Bible talks a lot about money and how to manage it:

- **Luke 14:28** – *"Suppose one of you wants to build a tower. Won't you first sit down and estimate the cost to see if you have enough money to complete it?"* That's budgeting—thinking ahead before making a move.
- **Proverbs 21:20** – *"The wise store up choice food and olive oil, but fools gulp theirs down."* That's saving—knowing when to hold onto what you have instead of spending it all as soon as it hits your account.
- **Proverbs 27:23-24** – *"Be sure you know the condition of your flocks, give careful attention to your herds."* That's knowing your assets—understanding what you have and taking care of it.

God has always emphasized *planning, managing,* and *protecting resources.*

A budget isn't just a financial tool—it's a way to manage what He's already put in your hands.

It's your personal plan for obedience, peace, and eventually... overflow.

Let's Talk About a Few Myths

We've all heard them—and maybe even believed them. But if we're going to move forward, it's time to let these go:

Myth: "I don't make enough to budget."

Truth: Actually? That's *exactly* why you need one. A budget helps you make the most of what you've got, no matter how much it is.

Myth: "Budgets are too strict."

Truth: Not true. You're the one creating it. You choose the categories, the priorities, the flexibility. This isn't financial jail—it's you taking charge.

Myth: "I'll start budgeting when I get a raise."

Truth: Let's flip that—budgeting is what helps you *keep* the raise when it comes. If you're not managing $500 well, more money won't fix it. It just magnifies what's already happening.

Prayer for Financial Clarity

Lord, thank You for being a God of order and wisdom. I no longer want to live in confusion or avoidance when it comes to my money. Teach me how to plan with purpose, spend with intention, and align my finances with Your will. Help me walk in clarity and discipline. Amen.

Action Steps

1. **Create your first real budget.** Keep it simple and realistic. Base it on your actual numbers.
2. **Notice your spending patterns this week.** Awareness creates clarity.
3. **Cut or adjust one area.** Look for one small shift that creates a little breathing room.
4. **Automate one thing.** Whether it's a bill or a savings transfer, set it and forget it. One less thing to think about.
5. **Speak this aloud each day:** *"I manage my money with wisdom, clarity, and purpose. I budget with God, not against Him."*

Reflection Questions

- What has been your attitude toward budgeting until now?
- Have you seen budgeting as helpful—or as something you "have to do" when things go wrong?
- What would financial peace look like for you?

A budget doesn't limit you. It gives your money direction—and when your money has direction, so does your life.

Chapter 3: You Are Not Lazy, You Are Unled

If you've ever called yourself lazy, I want to stop you right here.

You're not lazy. You're tired. You're overwhelmed.

You've been spinning your wheels, trying to stay afloat without a clear system, direction, or support. And now you're judging yourself for not being more productive in the middle of chaos.

That's not laziness.

That's a lack of leadership.

Many of us wear multiple hats—wife, mother, entrepreneur, career woman, and the list goes on. We stretch ourselves thin to make ourselves whole. I check many of the above boxes, so trust me—I get it. By the end of the day, I'm not just tired—I'm flat out exhausted. All I want to do is absolutely nothing.

After many failed attempts at organizing not just my finances, but my entire life, I finally realized the problem: I didn't have a system. I didn't have leadership over my time, my habits, or my money.

Most of us were never taught how to lead ourselves well. We were just told to work hard, hustle, and hope it pays off. But God didn't call you to survive through sheer effort—He called you to move with wisdom, order, and intention.

What the Ant Taught Me

I used to read Proverbs 6:6 and honestly feel a little defeated. Like—*great, even ants are better at managing life than I am.*

But one day, I slowed down and actually *listened* to what the verse was saying:

"It has no commander, no overseer, no ruler—yet it stores in summer and gathers in harvest."

And I realized something important: I kept waiting.

Waiting for motivation to magically show up.

Waiting for life to finally settle down.

Waiting for an emergency to force me into action.

But the ant doesn't wait for anyone. It doesn't need a reminder, or a deadline, or a crisis to keep moving. It has discipline built into its rhythm. It trusts the rhythm and timing God built into it.

That's when it clicked: I wasn't broken. I wasn't lazy. I just needed to *lead* myself.

I needed to become the woman who prepares *before* the storm ever shows up at the door.

The woman who trusts that God's timing is already at work—and moves with it.

Laziness vs. Lack of Structure

Laziness is when you know what needs to be done and you simply don't care enough to do it. But most of us do care—we're just stuck. We're exhausted, overwhelmed, and unsure of where to start.

You wake up with good intentions, but you don't have a plan. You get paid, but you don't have a system. You want to save, but you don't know what you're saving for—or how much you actually need.

It's not a character flaw. It's a planning gap. And the beautiful thing about a gap is that it can be filled. It can be fixed.

You're not failing—you're just missing a framework. And that's exactly what we're about to build together.

Signs You're Not Lazy—You're Just Unled

If any of this sounds familiar, you're not alone—and you're not lazy. You're simply operating without a system to lead you forward.

- You feel busy all the time but aren't seeing real progress.
- You start with good intentions but struggle to stay consistent.
- You carry guilt about money decisions but aren't sure how to change them.
- And more often than not, you're reacting to life instead of planning ahead.

These aren't signs of failure—they're signals that it's time to reclaim leadership over your life and your finances, with wisdom, structure, and God's help.

And the good news? You don't have to figure it out on your own.

What Scripture Says

God has a lot to say about discipline and preparation—and it's not about being perfect. It's about walking in wisdom.

- **Proverbs 6:6–8** – *"Go to the ant, you sluggard; consider its ways and be wise! It has no commander, no overseer or ruler, yet it stores its provisions in summer and gathers its food at harvest."* Preparation without being told. Self-discipline is a sign of spiritual maturity.
- **Proverbs 10:4** – *"Lazy hands make for poverty, but diligent hands bring wealth."* Diligence isn't optional – it's a direct path to increase.
- **1 Corinthians 14:40** – *"Let all things be done decently and in order."* Order is godly. Building structure in your life and finances reflects His nature.

This journey isn't about chasing perfection—it's about stewardship. When you get your house in order—even if it's just one drawer, one account, or one calendar—you start moving in rhythm with the way God designed you to live.

Prayer for Discipline & Direction

God, I know You are not the author of confusion. I ask that You help me lead my life with discipline, peace, and clarity. Teach me to plan with You, not apart from You. Help me build rhythms and habits that reflect Your wisdom and bring You glory. I'm ready to lead my life the way You intended. Amen.

Action Steps

1. **Create a rhythm, not just a routine.** Choose a consistent time each week to budget, reflect on your spending, and take care of bills. Let it become a natural part of your rhythm, not a rigid checklist.
2. **Take ownership of your financial leadership.** Choose a specific day each week to check in on your finances, review goals, and make any needed adjustments. Leading with consistency builds confidence and clarity.
3. **Declutter one space.** Choose one drawer, one shelf, one surface—and clear it. A clean space opens up your mind for clearer thinking, better choices, and stronger follow-through.
4. **Write down your top 3 financial priorities.** Not everything is urgent. Getting crystal clear on what matters most helps you move with purpose instead of pressure.
5. **Speak this over yourself daily:** *"I have the mind of Christ. I lead my time, habits, and money with wisdom and grace."*

Reflection Questions

- Where in your life do you feel most "lazy" right now?
- What structures or support would help you feel more in control?
- What would leadership over your life look like, practically?

You don't need a miracle to get organized. You need a plan, a little discipline, and a whole lot of grace.

Start leading your life—and watch how much easier it becomes to follow God's plan for it.

II

Part Two

The Purpose of Prosperity

"The plans of the diligent lead to profit as surely as haste leads to poverty." Proverbs 21:5

Chapter 4: Wealth Is Biblical – So Why Are We Afraid of It?

Let's talk about the burdens that too many of us carry:

We want financial freedom.

We want to provide for our families.

We want more than just scraping by

But deep down? We feel guilty for wanting it.

Somewhere along the line, someone convinced us that wanting wealth was selfish.

That abundance and faith couldn't coexist. That being "a good Christian" meant settling for less. But when you actually look at the Word, it says something very different.

God Created Abundance—Not Bare Minimums

Look at how God designed the Garden of Eden. There wasn't just *enough*—there was *overflow*. Rivers, gold, fruit, provision, purpose.

Adam wasn't struggling to "get by." He was called to tend to it, work it, care for it—not to struggle in it.

God *gave* that wealth. He *designed* it.

He wasn't offended by abundance—He created it.

So where did the fear come from?

Why We're Afraid of Wealth

For many women of faith, wealth feels dangerous because:

- We've seen it mishandled
- We were taught money is "worldly"
- We fear becoming prideful or disconnected from God
- We associate wealth with greed, exploitation, or selfishness

But here's the truth: money is not evil.

The love of money is.

If you build wealth on the foundation of stewardship, purpose, and faith, then money becomes a tool in the hands of someone submitted to God.

The Day I Realized God Wasn't Offended by My Goals

I remember sitting down one day and writing out a list of my financial goals:

- Pay off debt.
- Build a 6-month emergency fund.
- Start a business.
- Buy a home.
- Give to others in need.

I looked at the list... and I felt bad. Like I was being greedy or asking for too much.

But then I felt this very clear nudge from God:

"None of this is outside of My will—as long as your heart stays within My will."

And that moment shifted everything.

I stopped apologizing for wanting to break financial strongholds.

I stopped pretending that I was "fine" with struggle.

And I started seeing my goals as *assignments*, not selfishness.

What Scripture Says

If you've ever doubted whether God wants you to walk in overflow—not just survival—it's time to go back to the Word.

- **Deuteronomy 8:18** – *"But remember the Lord your God, for it is He who gives you the ability to produce wealth."* Wealth isn't self-made—it's God-given. That ability is a gift.
- **Proverbs 10:22** – *"The blessing of the Lord brings wealth, without painful toil for it."* When God blesses it, you don't have to burn out to build it.
- **Genesis 1:28** – *"Be fruitful and multiply... fill the earth and subdue it."* From the very beginning, God called us to grow and govern—not just survive.

Wealth isn't unholy. It's how we pursue it and what we do with it that matters.

Prayer to Release Guilt Around Wealth

Lord, I repent for believing that I wasn't allowed to desire more. I now understand that wealth, in Your hands, is good. Teach me to seek prosperity with humility, responsibility, and purpose. I release guilt and pick up grace. Make me a vessel You can trust. Amen.

Action Steps

1. **Write your personal wealth goals—don't censor them.** Let them stretch your faith.
2. **Match each goal with a purpose.** Why does it matter? Who does it impact?
3. **Identify any guilt or shame.** Where did those feelings come from? Is it aligned with what Scripture says?
4. **Read Deuteronomy 8 this week.** Let the Word reframe your mindset about provision and abundance.
5. **Speak this over yourself:** *I am not afraid of wealth. I pursue it with purpose, wisdom, and faith."*

Reflection Questions

- What messages about wealth shaped your early view of money?

- How have those beliefs limited your financial progress?
- What would wealth allow you to do that you currently can't?

Because here's the truth:
You were never meant to shrink your life to match your fears.
You were meant to expand—to overflow—to steward—to bless.
Wealth in the hands of a woman surrendered to God?
That's a powerful thing.

Chapter 5: You Can't Serve God and Be Broke on Purpose

Let's get something straight: God doesn't need you broke to prove your loyalty.

And being wealthy doesn't mean you've lost your soul.

Too many believers are caught in a false choice: Be broke and holy. Or be rich and lost.

But that's not the gospel.

That's fear dressed up like humility.

This Is Not About Worshiping Wealth

Let's be clear—we're not here to bow to bank accounts or worship wealth. That's idolatry, and it's dangerous. If money owns your decisions, controls your identity, or becomes your source of security—*that's a problem*.

But so is constantly living in survival mode. So is ignoring your bills and calling it "faith."

So is not preparing for the future and blaming the devil for what's really mismanagement.

There is no glory in lack when God has given you tools, wisdom, and the power to grow and build. He didn't call you to spiritualize dysfunction.

He called you to walk in wisdom.

Money Isn't the Master—It's the Assignment

God has a mission for your life. And whether that mission is to raise children, build a business, bless your community, or all of the above—it will take resources.

You can't say yes to the call if you're always stuck saying "not right now" to everything that costs. You can't pour out if you're financially empty. You can't give generously if you're barely scraping by. And most importantly, *you can't serve two masters.*

So here's the hard question: Are you letting money rule you by always being behind it?

Money doesn't have to be your idol to still have power over you.

And Jesus said it plainly: *You cannot serve both God and money.*

But notice—He didn't say you couldn't *use* money to serve God.

The Year I Realized I Was Living a Faith-Filled Lie

There was a season when I truly believed I was trusting God. I had no savings, barely paid my bills, and called it "walking by faith."

But if I'm honest? I wasn't walking by faith—I was walking without a plan.

I was spiritualizing my dysfunction and avoiding responsibility, hoping God would swoop in and fix it.

Eventually, I had to face the truth: I wasn't trusting God. I was just mismanaging what He had already given me.

God is faithful, but He's also a Father. And sometimes, the most loving thing He does is let the pressure stay long enough for us to change how we move.

What Scripture Says

If we want to walk in real freedom—freedom that honors God and stewards His blessings—we have to realign with what the Word says.

- **Matthew 6:24** – *"You can't serve two masters...You cannot serve both God and money."* Choose purpose over pressure.
- **Mark 8:36** – *"What good is it for someone to gain the whole world, yet forfeit their soul?"* Check your motives.
- **Ecclesiastes 5:10** – *"Whoever loves money never has enough."* Don't chase,

steward.

There's a middle path: Serving God fully. Using money wisely.
Refusing to be mastered by either fear or greed.

Prayer for Financial Integrity and Alignment

God, help me to serve You with my whole heart—not just with my praise, but with my money too. Align my desires with Your purpose. Help me break every tie to fear, greed, or pride. Teach me to use wealth as a tool for good, and to never bow to it as a master. Amen.

Action Steps

1. **Identify your current "master."** What's really driving your financial decisions—faith, fear, or pressure?
2. **Define your financial "why."** What role should money play in your purpose and calling?
3. **Set boundaries.** Where are you overspending to impress, escape, or compensate?
4. **Review your giving.** Does your generosity reflect your trust in God— or do you fear not having enough?
5. **Speak this over yourself:** *"Money doesn't master me. I use it wisely, give it freely, and serve God fully."*

Reflection Questions

- Have you ever avoided growth out of fear of "becoming too worldly"?
- What doors could open if you saw money as a servant—not a source of stress?
- In what areas of your life has financial fear been louder than faith?

God didn't call you to choose between Him and provision.
He called you to trust Him as your provider—and to walk in purpose

without being bound by lack.

You don't have to be broke to be righteous.

But you do have to be free.

Chapter 6: Faith in Action – Money That Reflects Mission

Let's talk about alignment. And not just the "get in position" kind.

I mean real alignment—the kind that shows up in your bank account, your spending habits, and your financial goals.

Because if your money doesn't reflect your mission... who is it really serving?

Faith Isn't Just What You Say—It's What You Do With Your Resources

It's easy to say "God first."

But if we pulled up your last 90 days of transactions, would that truth still hold?

- Are you giving with purpose or just out of guilt?
- Are you spending based on values or just convenience?
- Are you working toward a vision or just reacting to expenses?

Faith without works is dead.

And that doesn't just apply to prayer and action—it applies to belief and budgeting.

When your faith is real, it starts to shape how you manage money.

Your Budget Should Look Like Your Beliefs

If you say:

- "I want to build generational wealth." - Are you investing toward that?
- "I want to give more." - Is giving an actual line in your budget?
- "I want to honor God with my money." - Is that reflected in how you spend and save?

This isn't about perfection. It's about alignment.

It's about letting your dollars reflect your direction.

The Season I Was Earning More but Doing Less

There was a season when I was making more money than I ever had.

By every outside measure, I should have felt successful. But somehow I felt more off-track than ever before.

My giving was inconsistent. I was exhausted all the time. I was working long hours but rarely pausing to ask if any of it was helping me walk in my purpose.

I had the income. But I didn't have the impact.

When I finally slowed down enough to ask God what was going wrong, His answer was clear:

"It's not that you don't have enough. You're just not assigning what I gave you to what I called you to."

That was the moment I realized I didn't need more hustle. I needed more assignment-based stewardship.

I had to stop chasing goals—and start fulfilling assignments.

What Scripture Says

When you want realignment, the best place to start is with God's Word. It's there you'll find both the vision and the strategy.

- **Colossians 3:23–24** – *"Whatever you do, work at it with all your heart, as working for the Lord, not for human masters... It is the Lord Christ you are serving."* Do work from the heart that honors God. That includes how you earn and spend.
- **Matthew 6:33** – *"But seek first His kingdom and His righteousness, and all*

these things will be given to you as well." Prioritize God's mission—He'll take care of provision.

- **Proverbs 16:3** – *"Commit to the Lord whatever you do, and He will establish your plans."* When you surrender your plans, God secures your path.

Money was always meant to serve your mission—never to distract you from it.

Prayer for Alignment and Purpose

God, I want my money to reflect my faith. Show me where I've been spending without intention and building without You. Help me assign every dollar to the purpose You've designed for me. Teach me to budget with boldness, give with joy, and build with eternity in mind. Amen.

Action Steps

1. **Write your financial mission statement.** What do you want your money to accomplish spiritually, personally, and generationally?
2. **Review where your money has gone this past month.** Does it reflect your mission?
3. **Pick one habit to realign.** That could be tithing consistently, investing regularly, or tracking your giving. Choose one.
4. **Create "mission-driven" budget categories.** Add a giving line. A growth line. A legacy line. Let your budget speak the language of your mission.
5. **Speak this daily:** *"My money reflects my mission. I spend, save, and sow with intention."*

Reflection Questions

- What does a mission-aligned financial life look like for you?
- In what areas have you been spending without clarity or conviction?

- How could your finances create more impact if aligned with your faith?

Faith isn't just what you believe—it's how you behave. And your financial behavior is one of the loudest declarations of what you trust, value, and pursue.

It's time for your money to get in agreement with your mission.

Not just someday—but today.

III

Part Three

Building Like the Bible Says

"Now it is required that those who have been given a trust must prove faithful." 1 Corinthians 4:2

Chapter 7: Stewardship Is Sexy (Yes, I Said It)

Let's change the narrative: Stewardship is not boring. It's not old-fashioned. It's not something we do because we're broke or trying to "play it safe." Stewardship is bold. It's empowering. It's strategic. It's deeply spiritual. And yes—*it's sexy.*

Because there's nothing more attractive than a woman who knows what she has, values it, and multiplies it wisely.

This isn't about scarcity—it's about sacredness.

What God has placed in your hands deserves care, clarity, and commitment.

What Is Stewardship, Really?

Stewardship is not about how much you have. It's about how well you manage what you do have. It's the ability to:

- Plan with purpose instead of reacting out of pressure
- Prioritize what matters so everything doesn't feel urgent
- Track your money instead of wondering where it went
- Maximize what's in your hand instead of obsessing over what's not
- Protect what God has trusted you with—even when no one's watching

God doesn't bless recklessness. He blesses faithfulness.

If you've been praying for overflow but avoiding the hard truth of where your money actually goes…

You're not asking for a blessing. You're asking for a bailout.

The Season I Started Noticing the "Little Things"

I used to think I was being responsible because I paid the "big" bills on time.
Rent? Check. Car note? Check. Utilities? Got it.
But the little things? I ignored them.

1. A random $12 subscription I forgot to cancel
2. Late fees because I didn't double-check a due date
3. Coffee runs and small Target trips that added up and left me wondering, *"Where did all my money go?"*

Then one Sunday, I heard a sermon that changed my perspective.
It said, *"God is watching how you handle what seems insignificant to you."*
That was my wake-up call.
I realized if I couldn't manage $100 with discipline, why did I think I was ready for $100,000 with clarity?
That moment shifted something in me.
I stopped asking, *"Why don't I have more?"* and started asking, *"Am I managing what I already have?*

What Scripture Says

Scripture gives us a clear foundation for what stewardship really looks like:

- **Luke 16:10–11** – *"Whoever can be trusted with very little can also be trusted with much..."* This is about capacity. If you want to be trusted with more, start with what's already in your hands.
- **Luke 12:48** – *"From everyone who has been given much, much will be demanded..."* With blessing comes responsibility. God expects us to manage what we've been given with care and purpose.
- **1 Peter 4:10** – *"Each of you should use whatever gift you have received to serve others, as faithful stewards of God's grace in its various forms."* Stewardship isn't just about money—it's about using every resource, gift,

and opportunity for something greater than ourselves.

God gives seed to the sower—not the waster.

Why This Matters for Wealth-Building

You don't build wealth just by making more. You build it by learning how to keep more, grow more, and protect more. That's what stewardship is.

Not another side hustle. Not another manifestation affirmation. Not just more effort.

But real alignment: *Faith + Discipline + Stewardship = Increase.*

The women who build wealth on purpose are the ones who manage on purpose.

The ones who say, *"What I have right now is worthy of structure, attention, and gratitude."*

Prayer for Stewardship

God, thank you for trusting me with what I have. No matter how small or large it feels. Teach me to manage it with wisdom, care, and integrity. Help me to build systems and habits that honor You. Let my stewardship speak of my faith. And may my faithfulness be the seed You multiply. Amen.

Action Steps

1. **Do a weekly check-in to see where your money is flowing.** What needs adjusting?
2. **Audit subscriptions and auto-pays.** Small leaks sink big ships. Cancel what no longer aligns with your values or goals.
3. **Create a stewardship system.** Set up a basic method (spreadsheet, budget app, or notebook) where you track bills, giving, saving, and your goals.
4. **Build a habit of mindful review.** Set aside 15 focused minutes each week to check your account balances, track your progress, and prepare for upcoming responsibilities. A little attention goes a long way.

5. **Speak this aloud:** *"I am a wise and faithful steward. What I manage well, God multiplies."*

Reflection Questions

- What areas of your life are calling for more intentional stewardship right now—time, money, energy, relationships?
- What has God already placed in your hands that you could manage better?
- How would sharpening your stewardship today prepare you for the greater responsibility you've been praying for?

There's nothing small about the "small things."

Because how you manage them *is the test.*

And a woman who manages her life—and her money—with clarity, purpose, and care?

That's a woman walking in her assignment.

That's a woman ready for more.

Chapter 8: God's Blueprint for Generational Wealth

Let's talk about legacy.

Not just what happens after you're gone—but what you're intentionally building right now that will live beyond you.

Because in the Kingdom of God, wealth isn't just measured by what you make.

It's measured by what you leave.

Legacy is active. It's present-tense. It's the financial decisions, spiritual values, and intentional habits you shape today that will bless people you haven't even met yet.

God never meant for you to grind your whole life just to get by, only to leave your children with debt, trauma, or the burden of starting over.

He designed you to leave a blueprint. A blessing. A testimony.

What Is Generational Wealth—Really?

We hear the term thrown around a lot, but let's break it down. Generational wealth is more than money in a bank account. Its:

- Financial assets - cash, real estate, stocks, businesses, retirement plans
- Spiritual values - integrity, faith, purpose, discipline
- Knowledge - how to earn, save, invest, give, and grow
- Systems - budgets, life insurance, wills, estate plans
- Freedom - so your children don't have to start from scratch)

God doesn't bless you just for you.

When He gives you the ability to produce wealth (Deuteronomy 8:18), He's placing a responsibility in your hands—not just to enjoy it—but to multiply it for those coming after you.

The Moment I Realized My Ceiling Was Someone Else's Floor

For years, I thought wealth was about "making it"—paying bills, getting out of debt, trying to save a little. But then it hit me.

I didn't want my children to figure it out the hard way like I did. I didn't want them buried under the same weight I had to fight my way out of.

I thought back to the late nights I spent trying to repair credit. The stress of not knowing how to build savings. The confusion around investing and the overwhelm of financial literacy that I was never taught.

I had to fight to learn it all on my own. And I decided right then—I was going to be the *last generation* that had to start from scratch.

> *My ceiling will be their floor.*
> *My healing will be their history.*
> *And my discipline will be their inheritance.*

I vowed to teach my children early what I learned late.

To lay the foundation *now*—so they could build higher, faster, and with greater purpose.

That's when I realized: Wealth isn't just what you earn. It's what you equip the next generation to carry.

What Scripture Says

Scripture doesn't leave us guessing when it comes to wealth and inheritance. It gives us the blueprint for building something that outlives us:

- **Proverbs 13:22** – *"A good person leaves an inheritance to their children's children."* This isn't just wisdom—it's a spiritual principle. Legacy is part of the call.

40

- **Psalm 112:2–3** – *"Their children will be mighty in the land; the generation of the upright will be blessed. Wealth and riches are in their houses, and their righteousness endures forever."* Generational blessings aren't random. They are the fruit of righteousness and stewardship.
- **2 Corinthians 9:6–7** – *"Whoever sows generously will also reap generously."* Your sowing today isn't just for you. It's for every generation your life touches.

You were never meant to be the last link in the chain.

You were meant to be the bridge—from what was broken to what will be blessed.

This Starts With You

You can't pass on what you don't possess. You can't build a legacy on wishful thinking.

If your finances are a mess, your children will inherit the mess.

If you never build wealth, they'll inherit the weight of starting over.

And listen—this isn't about guilt. This is about *ownership*.

You have the power to break cycles and build systems.

You can change your family tree with one decision:

"I'm not leaving them with survival. I'm leaving them with strategy."

Prayer for Legacy and Generational Impact

Lord, I thank You for trusting me with the opportunity to build something that lasts. Give me wisdom, discipline, and vision to build not just for myself, but for those who come after me. Let my life reflect Your abundance, and may everything I build point back to You. Amen.

Action Steps

1. **Write your legacy vision.** Who are you building for? What do you want to leave behind—financially, spiritually, and practically?
2. **Start building tangible assets.** You don't need to do it all at once. One

investment, one savings goal, one business plan at a time.

3. **Teach what you know.** Your children, your nieces and nephews, your mentees—someone is watching you. Share what you're learning. Don't let the knowledge die with you.

4. **Create a will or trust.** Don't leave it to chance—put your legacy on paper.

5. **Speak this aloud:** *"I build wealth on purpose. My discipline now becomes blessing for generations later."*

Reflection Questions

- What legacy were you handed—and what needs to change?
- Who are you building for?
- What would it look like for your children to start with provision instead of *struggle*?

You don't need a million dollars to leave a legacy.

You need vision, wisdom, and a decision to start.

Because legacy isn't just about the wealth you accumulate.

It's about the wisdom you *activate*—for every generation coming behind you.

So start now.

Start here.

Build what they won't have to rebuild.

Chapter 9: The Tithe & The Overflow

Let's talk about tithing. Not the guilt-trip version. Not the "give it or else" version.

But real tithing.

Tithing is one of the most misunderstood and, let's be honest, most avoided financial practices in the faith. Some treat it like a spiritual tax. Others avoid it altogether, unsure if it's outdated or even biblical.

And then there are those of us who wrestled quietly—wondering:

"Where is this money really going?"

"Is the church even using it right?"

"Does God even care if I give it or not?"

My Honest Struggle with Tithing

I didn't always tithe. Not consistently. Not joyfully. And definitely not faithfully.

There were seasons when I gave whatever was left—if anything. And even then, I questioned it. I had bills to pay, mouths to feed, dreams to chase—tithing felt like just another line item on an already tight budget.

And the truth?

I wasn't tithing in faith. I was tithing in fear—when I did it at all.

I kept telling myself, *"I'll tithe when things get better."*

But eventually, I had to face the real test: *Would I trust God now? Or only when it felt safe?*

One day, I made the choice to tithe *first.* Not after the bills. Not after the plans. Not after the "what ifs."

I said, *"God, You get the first, not the leftovers."*

And that's when things started to shift.

No, money didn't fall from the sky. But I experienced something even more valuable:

A peace that didn't make sense.

Provision that showed up in ways I couldn't explain. Open doors I didn't knock on.

Wisdom I hadn't prayed for—but needed. Steady strength to keep going even when the numbers still looked tight.

God didn't just meet my needs—*He realigned my faith.* He showed me that tithing wasn't about money—it was about trust.

And when I put Him first, He took care of the rest.

What That Season Taught Me

Tithing wasn't a magic trick.It didn't erase every financial challenge overnight.

But it did unlock a different kind of wealth:

- Clarity in my decisions
- Calm in the chaos
- Confidence that God really is my Provider

What shifted wasn't just my budget—it was my belief.

I stopped seeing tithing as something I "had" to do, and started honoring it as something I *get* to do.

A way to put my faith into action.

A way to say with my wallet what I already believed in my heart: *"God, I trust You more than my paycheck."*

And that's when I finally understood—

Tithing isn't about what you give up.

It's about what you gain when you let God lead.

What Is a Tithe, and Why Does It Matter?

The word "tithe" literally means tenth. Biblically, it's about giving the first 10% of your income to God—often through your local church.

But it's not just about the numbers. It's about priority.

It's not, "Let me see what I have left."

It's, "Before anything else, God, I acknowledge You."

Tithing isn't paying a bill. It's making a statement:

"God, I trust You to take care of all of it—so I'm giving You the first part in faith."

What Scripture Says

The Word speaks directly to the heart behind giving:

- **Malachi 3:10** – *"Bring the whole tithe into the storehouse... Test me in this,"* *says the Lord Almighty, "and see if I will not throw open the floodgates of heaven..."* Tithing is one of the few places where God invites us to try Him—*on purpose.*
- **Luke 6:38** – *"Give and it will be given to you."* Your giving sets a divine cycle in motion—one of generosity, not loss.
- **Proverbs 11:24–25** – *"The world of the generous gets larger and larger."* This is spiritual economics. When you give, you grow—spiritually and practically.

Tithing isn't transactional. It's relational.

It's not about buying blessings—it's about aligning your heart with the Source of your provision.

When you give consistently, cheerfully, and with purpose—you shift from surviving to sowing.

And sowing always leads to overflow.

What About Offerings, Giving Beyond the Tithe?

An offering is anything you give beyond the tithe.

It's the "above and beyond" kind of giving—whether it's blessing someone in need, supporting a ministry, or responding to a tug God places on your heart.

It's not about how much you give. It's about the spirit in which you give it. You don't need to have extra to be generous. You just need a heart that's open and willing.

Prayer for a Generous and Trusting Heart

God, I want to honor You with my finances—not just in word, but in action. Help me trust You fully. Teach me to give with joy, not fear. Remind me that everything I have comes from You, and that You are my source. Make me a generous and faithful steward. Amen.

Action Steps

1. **Take an honest look at your giving patterns.** Have you been tithing faithfully, or waiting for "better timing"?
2. **Put your tithe first.** Don't wait until the end of the month. Automate it if you need to.
3. **Ask God where to give an offering.** Be sensitive to that nudge—it might not be flashy, but it's always purposeful.
4. **Document the faithfulness.** Keep a journal of how God shows up after you sow. You'll be amazed at the story He's writing.
5. **Speak this daily:** *"I give with purpose. I sow with faith. I receive with gratitude. Overflow belongs to me."*

Reflection Questions

- What emotions come up when you think about tithing?
- Have you ever experienced God provide after giving in faith?
- What would change in your life if you trusted God with your *first*—not your leftovers?

Tithing isn't about losing money.
It's about unlocking peace.
It's not about obligation. It's about alignment.

Because when your heart is aligned—He multiplies what you trust Him with.

And when you live with open hands—God fills them. Every time.

IV

Part Four

Walking It Out

"...that you may live a life worthy of the Lord and please him in every way: bearing fruit in every good work, growing in the knowledge of God." Colossians 1:10

Chapter 10: The Plan – Budgeting with Purpose

Let's talk about the B-Word: *budgeting.*

By now, you've probably noticed that we've talked about the word "budget" in almost every chapter.

That's no accident.

Budgeting is how faith becomes movement. It's how your prayers become plans.

It's how you stop living in reaction and start living in rhythm—with God and your goals.

A budget is more than a spreadsheet. It's a weapon. A guide.

A declaration that your money is going to serve you—not stress you out.

If you're serious about breaking cycles, building wealth, and honoring God with your finances, budgeting isn't optional.

It's essential.

Breaking the Budget Curse in My Family

Budgeting wasn't just new to me—it was new to my whole family.

We didn't grow up talking about budgeting. Nobody pulled out a spreadsheet after payday.

We just spent, prayed we'd make it to next week, and hoped nothing unexpected came up.

Not me. Not my mom. Not my dad. Not my siblings. Nobody budgeted.

But one year, we decided enough was enough.

As a family, we took on the challenge to learn how to budget—and not just for ourselves, but to change our legacy.

We sat down together, tracked every single dollar, and faced our spending with courage instead of shame.

That day changed everything.

We didn't just get on the same financial page. We *rewrote* the book.

We conquered one of our biggest generational hurdles as a team—and we refused to be victims of our dollars any longer.

For the first time, we had direction. We had confidence.

We saw our debt shrinking and our dreams expanding.

And we realized: *Budgeting doesn't just change your money. It changes your mindset.*

And when your mindset changes, your future opens up.

What Budgeting Really Is (and Isn't)

Let's clear something up: Budgeting is *not* punishment.

Budgeting is as much a spiritual practice as it is a financial one.

It's how you bring order to what God has given you.

It's how you tell your money where to go instead of wondering where it went.

It's not about restriction—it's about intention.

Budgeting is:

– A spiritual discipline

– A practical tool

– A form of leadership over your life

Because every dollar God entrusts to you has a purpose.

And budgeting? That's how you give it one.

What Scripture Says

The Bible doesn't tiptoe around money. God is a planner. He values order. And He expects us to steward what we're given with wisdom and purpose.

• **1 Corinthians 4:2** – *"Now it is required that those who have been given a* *trust must prove faithful."* Your money is a trust. Budgeting is faithfulness in action.

- **Proverbs 16:9** – *"In their hearts humans plan their course, but the Lord establishes their steps."* Planning isn't the opposite of faith—it's a partner to it. Make the plan, then let God guide it.
- **Habakkuk 2:2** – "Write the vision and make it plain…" When you put your financial vision on paper, you're no longer dreaming—you're directing your future with purpose.

God doesn't bless chaos. He blesses stewardship.

And budgeting is part of that stewardship.

Build a Budget That Reflects Your Life + Faith

A purpose-driven budget isn't just about paying bills—it's about building a life with intention. Building freedom. Creating breathing room. Growing wealth that aligns with your values.

Here's a simple framework to build a God-first budget:

- **Tithing** - Honor God with the first
- **Giving** - Overflow into others
- **Savings** - Prepare for the future
- **Investing** - Build long-term wealth
- **Bills/Essentials** - Care for needs
- **Freedom Fund** - Joy, rest, travel, hobbies
- **Growth** - Courses, books, learning
- **Debt Payoff** - Cancel what's holding you back

The key: make it fit *your* life—not what looks trendy online.

Your budget should serve your purpose—not someone else's aesthetic.

Prayer for Wisdom and Discipline in Planning

God, thank You for being a God of order and strategy. I want to honor You with how I plan, spend, and save. Give me clarity and discipline. Show me how to use my money with intention, not impulse. Help me stay focused on long-term vision, not short-term emotion. Amen.

Action Steps

1. **Create your first "God-first" budget.** Start where you are.
2. **Keep your weekly or biweekly budget date.** It creates momentum. And consistency creates clarity.
3. **Choose one short-term financial goal.** Pay off a bill. Save $300. Tithe consistently. Start small and build momentum.
4. **Include room for joy.** Your budget should have space for things that make you feel alive—not just responsible.
5. **Speak this aloud daily:** *"I budget with wisdom. I lead my money. I honor God through planning."*

Reflection Questions

- What's one new habit you could build into your budget this month?
- Where have you avoided planning due to fear, shame, or overwhelm?
- What would change in your life if you had full clarity and confidence with your money?

Budgeting isn't just a tool—it's a turning point.

It's how you say, *"This money has a mission."*

And when your money is on mission, your future gains momentum.

Plan boldly.

Lead wisely.

Budget faithfully.

Chapter 11: Investing Without Fear

When most people hear the word investing, they either get excited—or immediately feel overwhelmed.

Maybe it sounds too risky. Maybe it feels too complicated. Maybe you think you don't have enough money to even try.

But here's the truth: *Investing isn't just for Wall Street.* It's for women of wisdom, too.

It's for women who are ready to break cycles and build legacies.

It's for you.

God doesn't just want you to work hard for your money—He wants your money to work hard for *you*.

Not because you're chasing riches, but because you're walking in purpose.

You're called to multiply, not just survive.

And investing is a way of honoring that call.

From Missed Chances to Multiplying Seeds

I didn't grow up learning about investing.

Nobody pulled me aside to say, *"Here's how to grow your money. Here's how to build wealth the smart way."*

So for years, I didn't invest. And I missed out—on growth, on opportunity, on time I could never get back.

Why? Because I didn't know.

And truthfully? I didn't *seek* to know.

But once I did start learning…

Everything changed.

The first time I put money into an investment—not toward bills, not into a savings account, but a real investment—it felt strange.

Honestly? It felt risky. There was a voice in my head asking, *"Shouldn't you be using that money for something safer?"*

But I reminded myself: I wasn't doing this recklessly—I was doing it on purpose.

It wasn't just about me. It was about freedom. It was about faith.

And when I saw that first bit of growth—when I realized my money was now working for *me*—I felt a kind of empowerment I'd never experienced before.

I finally understood what God meant when He said, *"Be fruitful and multiply."*

This was multiplication in action.

This was stewardship.

Why So Many Women of Faith Avoid Investing

If we're being honest—there are reasons we hesitate:

- "I don't know where to start."
- "I'm afraid of losing everything."
- "I've never seen anyone in my family invest."
- "I need to get out of debt first."

These fears are valid. But they don't have to rule you.

You don't need a finance degree.

You don't need a six-figure income.

You don't need to know it all today.

You just need to start small, stay consistent, and stay informed.

What Scripture Says

God wants us to grow what we have and step into His abundance, and He provides the blueprint for doing just that.

- **Ecclesiastes 11:1–2** – *"Ship your grain across the sea; after many days you* *may receive a return."* Spread out your investments. Diversify for safety and growth.

- **Proverbs 13:11** – *"Dishonest money dwindles away, but whoever gathers money little by little makes it grow."* Wealth gained little by little grows over time.
- **Proverbs 21:5** – *"The plans of the diligent lead to profit..."* Diligent planning leads to profit. Not gambling. Not guessing. Strategy.

Investing isn't worldly—it's wise.

It's not about getting rich quick. It's about building with intention and multiplying what God has given you.

Simple Types of Investing to Explore

You don't have to do them all. Just choose one to begin.

- **Stock Market** - Start with index funds or ETFs. Let your money grow with the market.
- **Retirement Accounts** - 401(k), IRA, or Roth IRA—plant seeds for your future.
- **Real Estate** - Buy property, earn rental income, or build equity over time.
- **Business Investing** - Build your own income-producing assets.
- **Micro-Investing Apps** - Apps like Acorns, Robinhood, or Fidelity let you start with just a few dollars.

Prayer to Overcome Fear and Build Wisdom

God, thank You for trusting me with the ability to grow what You've placed in my hands. Help me to make decisions guided by wisdom, not fear. Give me clarity, patience, and discernment as I build for the future. I want to be a faithful steward—multiply through me. Amen.

Action Steps

1. **Choose one area to begin learning about.** Watch a video, read a book, or talk to someone you trust.
2. **Start small.** Even $10/month into an investment account is a seed.
3. **Review your investments monthly or quarterly to stay on track.**
4. **Set a long-term goal.** Retirement, income replacement, or leaving a legacy.
5. **Speak this over yourself:** *"I do not fear money. I invest with wisdom. I grow with purpose. I build with faith."*

Reflection Questions

- What fears have kept you from investing in the past?
- What's one small step you can take this week toward your first (or next) investment?
- How would investing help you create freedom, not just for you—but for future generations?

You don't have to be perfect. You don't have to wait until you "have more."

You just have to begin.

Because when you invest in your future, you're aligning with God's vision of growth, overflow, and purpose.

And the reward?

Fruit that lasts.

Legacy that multiplies.

Freedom that glorifies God.

Chapter 12: Wealth with Vision – What Are You Really Building?

Let's pause and ask the question that changes everything: *What are you really building?*

Because money by itself isn't a purpose. It's not the goal. It's a tool.

A powerful one—when it's aligned with your mission.

You weren't created just to chase wealth. You were created to *build legacy*.

To create impact. To live on purpose—and leave something that outlives you.

The Shift That Changed Everything for Me

There was a time when all I thought about was getting by.

I had financial goals—but they were all about *survival*:

- "Pay off this card."
- "Make rent."
- "Save a little something—anything."

And that was a necessary start.

But one day, something in me woke up. I looked at my daughters and realized:

I didn't want them to start where I started.

I wanted their futures to be secure. I wanted them to have options, to follow their purpose without the weight of financial lack.

I didn't want money to be a barrier for them—I wanted it to be a bridge.

That's when I realized: *this isn't just about me.*

This is about my legacy. My great-great-great grandchildren.

The generations I'll never meet—but who will walk through doors I opened.

I knew then that I would be the last generation to not understand how to build wealth—

and the *first* to build a legacy that lasts.

So I started moving differently. Speaking differently. Spending and saving with *intention.*

Because once I understood this was bigger than me, my goals got bolder than my fears.

I went from:

- "Just get through the month," to "Build a business my kids can inherit."
- "Maybe one day I'll give more," to "I *am* the answer to someone's need—today."
- "Avoid debt," to "Own assets that grow while I sleep."

My money started moving in the direction of my mission.

And the more I aligned my goals with God's purpose, the clearer everything became.

What Makes It Kingdom wealth?

Kingdom wealth isn't just about how much you have—

It's about what you do with what you have.

It looks like:

- Lifting people out of poverty
- Funding ministries and businesses that serve
- Freeing your family from generational cycles
- Giving boldly and consistently
- Glorifying God, not self

You weren't created to just make money. You were created to multiply meaningfully.

To build something heaven recognizes.

What Scripture Says

God is clear—real wealth isn't just about accumulation. It's about building what will outlive you:

- **Matthew 6:19–20** – *"Do not store up for yourselves treasures on earth... But store up for yourselves treasures in heaven."* Don't store up temporary treasures. Focus on what lasts.
- **Philippians 4:19** – *"And my God will meet all your needs according to the riches of his glory in Christ Jesus."* God will meet your needs so you can stay focused on *His* purpose.
- **Proverbs 29:18** – *"Where there is no vision, the people perish..."* Visionless money vanishes. Wealth needs direction—and that starts with purpose.

God's not against wealth. He's against misplaced trust.

When your money aligns with your mission, it becomes more than income—it becomes impact.

How to Set Kingdom Wealth Goals

Ask yourself:

1. What is God calling me to build or support?
2. What kind of resources will that take?
3. What systems or habits will I need to maintain it?
4. Who will benefit from this beyond me?
5. What's stopping me—and what can I do about it this year?

Prayer for Vision-Driven Wealth Building

God, I don't want to build for vanity or validation. I want to build for Your glory. Help me clarify my goals so they align with Your Kingdom. Give me courage to dream big, and discipline to follow through. Let everything I create point back to You and bless those around me. Amen.

Action Steps

1. **Identify your top 3 Kingdom wealth goals—the impact you want your money to make.** Focus on vision, not just numbers.
2. **Make a plan for each.** Break it down into small, doable steps. Start where you are.
3. **Review monthly.** Keep your vision in front of you. Track the small wins.
4. **Pray for alignment.** Ask God to reveal if anything needs to shift—then move with obedience.
5. **Speak this aloud:** *"I am building wealth that blesses others, honors God, and leaves a legacy of faith and freedom."*

Reflection Questions

- Are your financial goals driven by fear, ego, or purpose?
- What part of your financial vision feels most aligned with God's bigger plan?
- Who will your wealth impact 10, 20, or even 50 years from now?

You weren't meant to just *work* and *hope*.

You were meant to *build* with purpose and walk out the mission God gave you.

So dream big.

Plan well.

And build boldly.

Because the vision inside you?

It's not too much.

It's *just the beginning.*

V

Part Five

Real Life & Real Love

"Two are better than one, because they have a good return for their labor: If either of them falls down, one can help the other up."
Ecclesiastes 4:9–10

Chapter 13: Money + Marriage – When Two Become One

Let's talk about one of the most sacred—and most sensitive—money relationships: *marriage.*

No matter how strong the love is, if the money isn't aligned, the marriage will feel strained.

And that doesn't mean you're doomed—it just means it's time to get intentional.

Because when two people become one, their finances need to reflect that oneness.

Not perfection.

Not identical spending habits. But shared values, shared vision, and shared responsibility.

Becoming One—Financially and Spiritually

Early on in our marriage, my husband and I realized we were trying to do something completely new—for both of us.

We hadn't grown up seeing wealth built. We hadn't seen budgeting modeled well.

We hadn't watched two people come together and build a financial future on purpose.

So we looked at each other and made a decision:

Let's give each other grace while we figure this out.

We started slow. We tried budgeting methods—several of them.

We made some really poor financial decisions. We got into debt... and praise God, we also got out of it.

We've experienced financial highs and lows, seasons of overflow and seasons where the numbers didn't quite add up.

But through it all, two things kept our marriage steady: *our faith in God, and our faith in each other.*

We knew there was a purpose bigger than the struggle.

We knew that unity didn't mean we'd always agree—it meant we'd always return to each other.

And once we got married, we stopped saying *"I"* and started saying *"we."*

Not just emotionally. Not just spiritually. But *financially.*

Why Money Creates Tension in Marriage

Most of the tension around money doesn't actually come from the math. It comes from:

- Different upbringings (spender vs. saver)
- A lack of communication or financial transparency
- Power dynamics around who earns more
- Past money wounds (debt, shame, control)
- Competing priorities or unclear financial goals

Money doesn't cause division—miscommunication about money does.

And if God isn't leading the conversation, fear usually will.

The Moment I Realized Unity Meant More Than Agreement

I'll be honest—there was a time I tried to "convince" my husband that my way of handling money was the right way.

I had the spreadsheets, the verses, the long explanations.

But he wasn't responding how I thought he should.

And that frustrated me—until I realized something.

Unity doesn't mean having the same approach.

It means having the same mission.

Marriage isn't about one person convincing the other. It's about learning, adjusting, and building *as one*.

When we made space for *prayer*, *planning*, and *honest conversations*—not lectures—peace followed.

What Scripture Says

God created us for partnership, and the Bible lays out the path to walk in unity and purpose.

- **Amos 3:3** – *"Can two walk together unless they are agreed?"* Agreement creates direction. Without unity, there's confusion. With unity, there's momentum.
- **Ecclesiastes 4:9–12** – *"Two are better than one, because they have a good return for their labor... If either falls, one can help the other up... A threefold cord is not easily broken."* Partnership multiplies strength. It's not just about support—it's about shared return and resilience.
- **Proverbs 24:3–4** – *"By wisdom a house is built, and through understanding it is established; through knowledge its rooms are filled with rare and beautiful treasures."* A strong home starts with wisdom. It grows through understanding and flourishes through shared vision.

Marriage is not just romantic—it's *strategic*.

It's a covenant of purpose.

And when you're aligned in your finances, your home becomes a strong foundation for faith, family, and legacy.

Practical Tools for Financial Unity

Here are some tools to strengthen both your hearts and your bank accounts:

- **Monthly Money Meetings** - Set a regular, pressure-free time to talk about bills, goals, giving, and financial wins—together.
- **A Shared Budget** - Even if you manage day-to-day expenses separately, your vision should be shared.

- **A Family Vision Statement** - What are you building? Agree on the mission, then let the money serve that mission.
- **A Safe Space to Disagree**- Not every decision will be easy. Create room to talk through disagreements, not avoid them.
- **Pray Together About Money** - Invite God into every financial conversation. Unity starts in His presence.

Prayer for Financial Unity in Marriage

Lord, thank You for the gift of partnership. Help us walk together in agreement and purpose. Teach us to listen, share, and make decisions in wisdom and grace. Let our finances reflect our faith and our future. May our home be filled with peace, provision, and unity. Amen.

Action Steps

1. **Schedule a financial check-in together.** Keep it honest, judgment-free, and full of hope.
2. **Create a list of shared financial goals.** Include short-term goals (saving for a trip) and long-term ones (debt freedom, legacy planning).
3. **Choose your financial system.** Joint, split, or hybrid—what matters most is clarity, consistency, and communication.
4. **Commit to one financial habit together.** Whether it's saving, giving, or paying down a bill—walk it out as one.
5. **Speak this together:***"We walk in unity. We build together. We honor God with our finances as one."*

Reflection Questions

- What's one thing you admire about how your spouse handles money?
- Where do you feel misaligned—and what would it take to get closer?
- What would financial peace in your marriage look like and feel like?

Money doesn't have to divide your marriage.

When two people align financially, spiritually, and purposefully—
they don't just survive marriage… they build something eternal.
With humility, communication, and God in the center—
your marriage can be a testimony of grace, growth, and generational impact.

Chapter 14: Breaking Generational Curses Without the Broke Talk

You've probably heard the phrase "breaking generational curses" a hundred times by now.

We say it with pride. We say it with urgency. We say it because we've *lived* through the pain of what came before us.

But here's the part that doesn't get talked about enough: *You don't have to stay broke to prove that you broke the curse.*

And you don't have to carry bitterness to build a better future. Breaking cycles doesn't mean repeating the pain with a new name.

It means replacing it—with wisdom, wealth, and wholeness.

What Is a Generational Curse, Really?

It's not superstition. It's not some mystical chain.

It's a *pattern*—passed down through beliefs, behaviors, mindsets, and consequences like:

- Chronic debt
- Financial secrecy or shame
- Scarcity mentality
- Avoidance of planning or building
- Normalized dysfunction and survival mode

You're not imagining the weight of it. But you don't have to carry it another step.

Because through Christ, you're no longer bound by it.

You've been redeemed. Now it's time to live like it.

The Day I Stopped Using My Past as a Limitation

For a long time, I used to say, *"No one ever taught me about money."*

And that was true. I didn't grow up seeing anyone invest.

There were no talks about generational wealth. Nobody showed me how to budget, save, or plan. But at some point, I realized:

That truth had become my excuse.

I was using it to justify habits that were holding me back. Every time I avoided facing my finances, I blamed what I didn't learn.

Then one day I heard something that stopped me cold:

> *"You're not responsible for the dysfunction you inherited.*
> *But you are responsible for not passing it on."*

That was the moment everything shifted.

I stopped trying to *distance* myself from my past and started deciding who I would become next. I stopped being angry at what I didn't receive and started becoming the person who builds what never existed in my family line.

It wasn't overnight.

There were tears, setbacks, and moments I wanted to give up.

But every time I chose healing over bitterness, wisdom over avoidance, and faith over fear—I was building legacy.

And not just for me.

For my children.

Their children.

And their children after them.

What Scripture Says

God has *always* been in the business of turning broken lines into blessed legacies:

- **Exodus 20:5–6** – *"I will show love to a thousand generations of those who love me and keep my commandments."* He extends love to a thousand generations. Your obedience today unlocks blessing tomorrow.
- **Galatians 3:13–14** – *"Christ redeemed us from the curse of the law..."* Christ redeemed us from the curse. The curse is broken—but the *systems* need to be rebuilt.
- **Proverbs 18:21** – *"The tongue has the power of life and death..."* Life and death are in the power of the tongue. Speak life over your story, your family, and your future.

God doesn't want you stuck in cycles of survival.

He wants you to build systems of *stability, abundance, and legacy.*

You Can Be the First... Without Being Bitter
You can be:

- The first to invest
- The first to tithe consistently
- The first to talk about money with your children
- The first to build wealth, own property, or create a will
- The first to dream beyond survival

But being "the first" doesn't mean being *perfect* or *prideful.*

It means being willing.

Willing to unlearn.

Willing to forgive.

Willing to walk a path you've never seen, because you know someone coming after you needs it.

Prayer for Healing, Release, and Redemption
God, thank You for giving me the strength to break what didn't honor You in my family line. I release the shame, anger, and fear tied to my financial past. I receive Your grace to build something new—freely, faithfully, and boldly.

Let my life reflect restoration, not resentment. Amen.

Action Steps

1. **Identify the financial patterns you inherited.** Which ones do you want to carry forward? Which ones stop with you?
2. **Create your new family blueprint.** What are the values, habits, and systems you're building from here?
3. **Speak differently.** Trade "we've always struggled" for "we are walking in wisdom and wealth."
4. **Choose forgiveness.** Not for their sake—but for your freedom.
5. **Speak this aloud:** *"I am not bound by the past. I am building a legacy of wisdom, wealth, and wholeness."*

Reflection Questions

- What financial wounds or patterns from your upbringing still affect you today?
- What are you building now that your family never had?
- How can you break cycles with grace and vision, instead of shame and fear?

Breaking generational curses isn't about being angry at the past.
It's about being faithful with the future.
You are not the problem.
You are the turning point.
And with God as your foundation, you won't just break the cycle—
You'll build the blueprint.

Chapter 15: When You Fall Off – Grace and Rebuilding Financially

Sometimes... you fall off.

You overspend. You miss a tithe. You swipe the credit card—*again.* You avoid the budget like it's judging you.

And the guilt creeps in fast. That inner voice starts whispering:

"See? You're not good with money."

"You've already messed up—why bother trying again?"

"You'll never get ahead."

But hear this loud and clear: One misstep doesn't cancel your mission. Falling off doesn't mean you're finished.

The Month I Gave Up (and the Day I Got Back Up)

There was a season when I was drowning in bills, debt, and unmet financial needs.

I was overwhelmed. I felt like I was doing everything "right"—but still falling behind.

So eventually... I just gave up.

I stopped budgeting.

I stopped checking balances.

I ignored the bills stacking up.

I didn't want to face it anymore. I felt *defeated.* Like everything I had worked so hard for had slipped through my fingers.

I told myself, *"You're back at square one."*

And the shame? It was heavy.

But here's the thing: It would've been easy to keep spiraling. To keep pretending. To let it all go and just live in survival mode again.

But one day, I made a choice.

Not a grand, perfect, everything-fixed-today choice—

Just a quiet decision to stop spiraling and *start again.*

So I started over.

I pulled out my notebook. I looked at the mess—not to beat myself up, but to *face it with honesty.*

I made a simple plan. I started small.

And I started chipping away at the damage with a stronger resolve than before.

This time… I knew where I went wrong.

I knew what didn't work.

And I came back with a better system, a clearer strategy, and a renewed sense of faith.

Why Shame Is a Trap, Not a Tool

Shame is sneaky. It doesn't just highlight what went wrong—it attacks *who you are.*

It tells you that because you messed up, you must be a mess.

It whispers:

- "You're just not good with money."
- "You'll never get it right."
- "You're behind everyone else."

But God doesn't use shame to change us—*He uses grace.*

And grace isn't permission to be reckless.

It's the power to get back up with wisdom and humility.

You don't need perfection.

You need progress.

You need patience.

And you need faith that refuses to quit, even when it feels like you're starting over—again.

What Scripture Says

Maybe you've made mistakes. Maybe you've fallen short. But falling isn't the end of your story—especially not with God.

- **Proverbs 24:16** – *"Though the righteous fall seven times, they rise again..."* Strength isn't in never falling. It's in refusing to *stay* down.
- **Lamentations 3:22–23** – *"Because of the Lord's great love we are not consumed, for his compassions never fail. They are new every morning..."* God's mercies are new every morning. Not just when you're doing great—*every* morning.
- **Micah 7:8** – *"Do not gloat over me, my enemy! Though I have fallen, I will rise."* That's not just scripture—it's a declaration.

You may feel behind. But grace always puts you back in position.

How to Rebuild Without Shame

Let's take the power back—not just from the bills, but from the guilt. Here's how to rebuild with wisdom:

1. **Name the moment.** Be honest about what happened—no sugarcoating, no beating yourself up.
2. **Return to your plan.** Revisit your budget, your goals, and your *why*. If it feels too big—simplify.
3. **Adjust with grace.** Maybe this month looks different. That's okay. A paused debt payment isn't failure. A smaller savings goal isn't defeat. It's *real life*.
4. **Reconnect with God.** Don't just ask for provision—ask for *peace*. He's not disappointed in you. He's *right beside you*, ready to help you start again.

Prayer for Rebuilding After Setbacks

God, thank You for being patient with me—even when I fall short. I release shame, fear, and guilt about my finances. I receive Your grace and wisdom to rebuild. Remind me that failure doesn't define me—faith does. Help me rise again, with clarity and courage. Amen.

Action Steps

1. **Take financial inventory.** What's changed? What's missing? What needs an update?
2. **Choose one thing to fix this week.** Start with a small win—cancel a subscription, pay a bill, update your budget.
3. **Rewrite your affirmation.** Take the lie you've been repeating and replace it with truth and scripture.
4. **Reach out for support.** Talk to someone—a coach, mentor, or trusted friend. You don't have to do this alone.
5. **Speak this daily:** *"Falling doesn't disqualify me. I rise with grace, wisdom, and divine strategy."*

Reflection Questions

- What story are you telling yourself when you fall off financially?
- How can you show yourself the same grace God shows you?
- What would rebuilding from a place of wisdom—not shame—look like?

You're not broken. You're rebuilding.

You're not too far gone. You're right on time for grace.

And this journey isn't over just because it got hard—

It's just getting started.

Outro: Your Yes is the First Investment

You made it.

You didn't just read a book on faith and finances—you said yes to living differently.

But let's be honest. Change doesn't happen just because you read the pages. It happens the moment you decide to *live* them.

The moment you said yes to:

- Trusting God with your money
- Breaking the cycles that tried to break you
- Choosing purpose over panic
- Learning instead of avoiding
- Starting small instead of staying stuck

That yes?

It was your first investment.

Not into a stock.

Not into a business.

But into *you*.

The version of you that God has been calling— the one who's equipped, positioned, and ready to build wealth with wisdom, walk boldly in purpose, and bless others from a place of overflow.

The Journey Is Just Beginning

You might still feel unsure. You might not have it all figured out.

And that's okay.

Faith doesn't demand perfection—it demands movement.

Maybe your next move is:

- Sitting down to create your first real budget
- Having an honest money conversation with your spouse
- Forgiving yourself for the financial past you can't change
- Starting to tithe again—no matter the amount
- Putting $10 into a savings account and naming it "seed"

Whatever it is—do it.

Not when you feel more ready.

Not when you feel more worthy.

Do it now.

Because your obedience in the present is how God unlocks blessings in the future.

What You're Building Matters

You're not just chasing numbers or goals.

You're changing the story.

You're shifting generations.

You're restoring what was broken.

You're walking by faith and not by fear.

You're living like you believe God meant what He said when He promised provision, abundance, and peace.

And all of that began with your yes.

Final Prayer

Lord, thank You for meeting me in these pages. Thank You for the truth, the clarity, the conviction, and the grace. Help me to walk in everything You've called me to financially—with wisdom, discipline, purpose, and joy. Let my life reflect what I've learned, and let my journey be a testimony of Your faithfulness. From this moment forward, I say yes. Yes to freedom. Yes to faith. Yes to purpose. Yes to legacy. Amen.

Final Reflection Questions

- What is one truth from this book that changed how you view money and faith?
- What's the first step you'll take toward financial purpose this week?
- Who do you know that needs this message—and how can you share it with them?

Your story isn't over.

Your resources aren't random.

And your money isn't meaningless.

You've said yes.

Now go live like it—*on purpose, in purpose, for His Kingdom.*